BACKYARD BIRDS

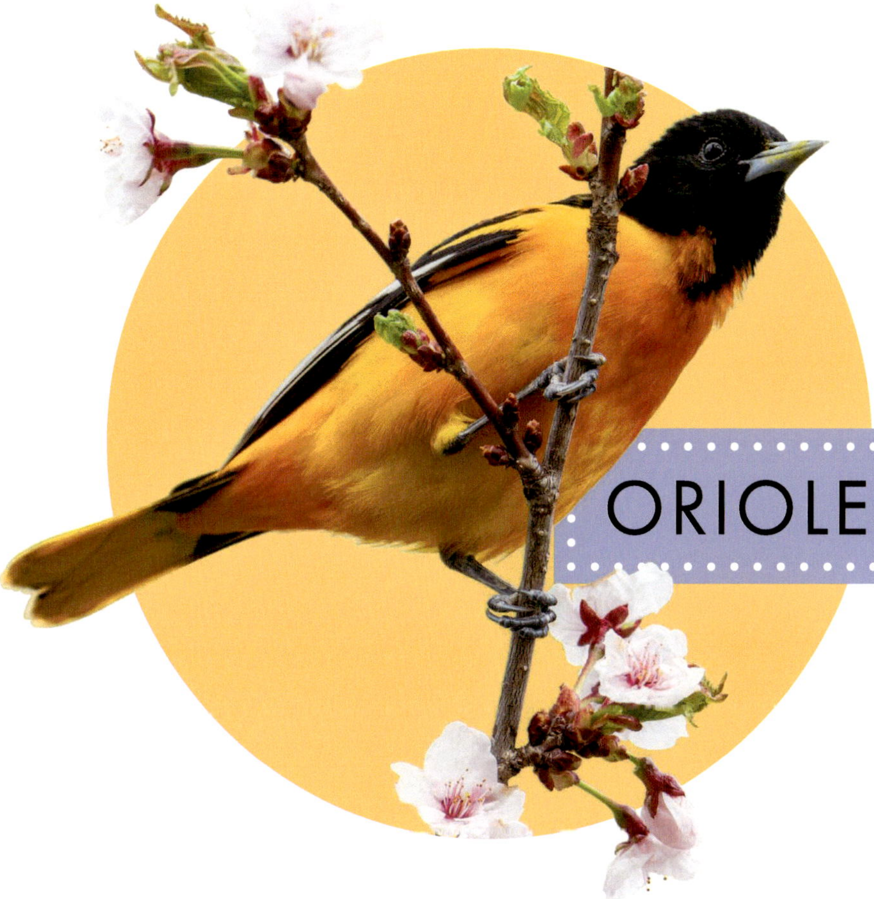

ORIOLES

by Anastasia Suen

nest

chicks

Look for these words and pictures as you read.

jelly

bill

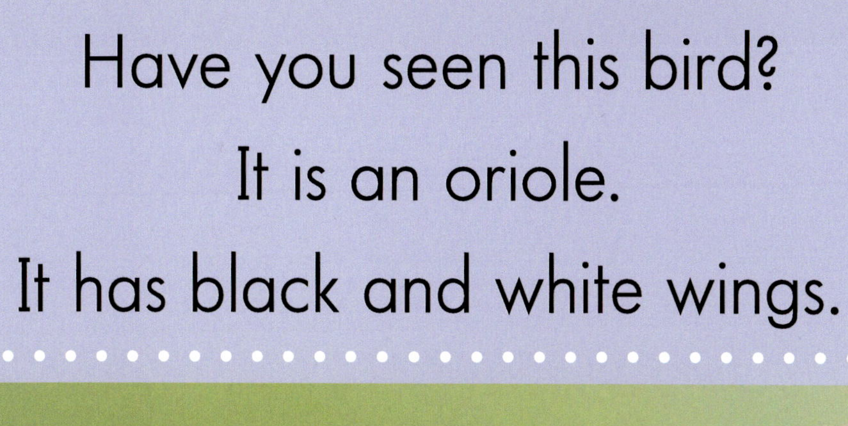

Have you seen this bird?

It is an oriole.

It has black and white wings.

Dads have a black head.
They have orange feathers.
Moms have yellow feathers.

Mom makes a nest.
She uses bark and vines.
It hangs from a tree.

nest

It is summer.
New chicks are born.
Mom feeds them bugs.

chicks

These birds love fruit.
They even eat grape jelly.
They find it at bird feeders.

jelly

bill

This bird drinks orange juice.
It uses its bill like a straw.

An oriole is a backyard bird.
Have you seen it?

nest

chicks

Did you find?

jelly

bill

Spot is published by Amicus Learning, an imprint of Amicus
P.O. Box 227, Mankato, MN 56002
www.amicuspublishing.us

Library of Congress Cataloging-in-Publication Data
Names: Suen, Anastasia author
Title: Orioles / by Anastasia Suen.
Description: Mankato, MN : Amicus Learning, an imprint of Amicus, [2026] | Series: Spot backyard birds | Audience: Ages 4–7 | Audience: Grades K–1 | Summary: "Orioles are small orange and black birds found across North America. This search-and-find book reinforces new vocabulary words with simple facts and compelling photographs to teach kindergarten and first grade readers about backyard birds"— Provided by publisher.
Identifiers: LCCN 2025010586 (print) | LCCN 2025010587 (ebook) | ISBN 9798892008334 library binding | ISBN 9798892008990 paperback | ISBN 9798892009652 ebook
Subjects: LCSH: Orioles—Juvenile literature
Classification: LCC QL696.P2 S8287 2026 (print) | LCC QL696.P2 (ebook) | DDC 598.8/74—dc23/eng/20250723
LC record available at https://lccn.loc.gov/2025010586
LC ebook record available at https://lccn.loc.gov/2025010587

Printed in United States of America

Ana Brauer, editor
Deb Miner, series designer
Sara Hood, book designer and photo researcher

Photos by Alamy Stock Photo/Kimberly Kotzian, 2, 12–13, 15, Linda Freshwaters Arndt, 2, 6–7, 15; Getty Images/imageBROKER/Rainer Mueller, 3, Yaorusheng, 2, 8–9, 15; Shutterstock/Gerald A. DeBoer, 14, Guoqiang Xue, 1, Linda McKusick, 2, 11, 15, Martin Pelanek, cover, 16, Mr.Coffee, 4–5